My Father's Daughter

Lily Lawson

Published by

THE
WRIGHT HOUSE

By the author

Poetry

My Father's Daughter

A Taste of What's to Come

Rainbow's Red Book of Poetry

https://www.lilyswritinglife.com/

Contents

Autopsy

I need my words ripped
and torn to shreds,
to have each remark
examined and questioned,
under the microscope,
if time allows.

To test myself against
whatever standards
you will set or use,
to see if I can meet them
or by some chance overcome,
or try again.

I want to evoke
some feeling in you,
that you maybe
have no language
to express,
yet you must try.

I want to touch you,
not with my hands,
but with my words.
To give rise to old thought
or even to create new,
that you may be changed.

If, as time moves on,
the words that I have shared
remain with you,
and call you back
to read them once again
my work is done.

One Breath

My lack of punctuation
can cause exasperation
and leave a person
quite gasping for air
the end result it seems
is to see how many reams
can be read in just one breath
like it's a dare
the need is to punctuate
so that one can hesitate
before continuing with
whatever happens next
I am guilty in my writing
of punctuation not inviting
but I can be even worse
within a text

My Favourite Vase

I have come to rely on you;
your weight, your capacity.
That you will welcome our flowers,
in your height and roundness.
That your heaviness, that threw me off balance at
our first meeting,
is a strength, belying your fragility.

You take centre stage,
happily sharing the limelight
with your temporary co-stars,
of varied persuasion
knowing your place is secure
in our affections,
while they are subject to replacement
once past their best.

The intricate patterns
of your crystal exterior
reflect the shafts of light
through my window,
casting ever-changing rainbows
in the daylight hours.
In the dark, you hide your magic,
your secret kept,
until revealed
by the sun.

LBD

My first and last little black dress
I am not a dress type girl.
This was the exception,
it fitted in a way I liked.

At the time, it represented me,
who I wanted to be,
who I thought I was,
who I will never be.

Back then, I tried on identities,
trying to fit the mould,
trying to be who they wanted,
trying to belong.

I could play the role,
I was comfortable, in a way,
but it took so much effort,
I am a low maintenance girl.

IPOD

You speak to me of unity.
A reminder that she loves me,
on the days that I doubt.
The unrepeatable
single act of peace.

You are the Tardis.
My companion on my travels.
Unnoticeable, unless in use.
Random like my thoughts.
You're classic gold.

In use you make me smile,
or sometimes cry.
Every minute has meaning.
You are a barrier
between me and the world

Your value is priceless.
You are irreplaceable.
The words you bestow
illustrate your originality.
You give me hope.

A Chance to Dance

I can't remember life without you
and I know you'll never leave.
You celebrate my happiness
and help me when I grieve.
You sometimes reach into my soul
and make me want to cry.
I know I can return to you
until the day I die.
You cheer me up,
you speak to me,
you make me want to dance.
I love you for eternity,
I'm just glad to have the chance.

The Door of Emotion

You slam in anger,
shaking the foundations,
our frustrations expressed.

You close quietly in grief,
standing like a barrier between us,
we are, to each other, unreachable.

You are the jailer,
keeping us under lock and key,
taking away our freedom.

You open in greeting,
to friend, family, and stranger,
with happiness, joy, or acceptance.

You keep us safe from the world,
our protector and shield,
in the dark hours of night.

Darkness

O bring the darkness on
and let it hide from me,
the things the like of which,
I do not wish to see.

In its all-encompassing arms
I feel forever free,
that I can at last become
who I wish myself to be.

In daylight observation,
I'm under pressure to conform,
as the darkness beckons,
I no longer feel so torn.

Some spend the night time hours,
waiting for the coming dawn,
but in the throes of darkness,
I can feel myself reborn.

The Church Hall

I walk through familiar doors
never knowing what I'll find,
the joy of sharing spaces
is that no one shuts the blind.

The sunlight through the windows,
catches me unawares,
despite noises to the contrary,
there's nobody upstairs.

The notice boards are very full
but somewhat out of date,
I know now if I check
there'll be rubbish by the gate.

The ticking clock is all I hear
as I am here alone.
Sometimes while I'm busy,
there will be a ringing phone.

The cupboard doors are straining
to keep the contents in,
soon the room will fill with people,
and the chaos will begin.

Sunday Rain

Sunday rain falls on the quiet street.
Holes in the tarmac fill with water,
reflecting buildings in bite size pieces,
emptiness the reminder of the day.

The old familiar structure of the week,
abruptly left without a backward glance.
Lack of identity leaves me lost,
unable to tell one day from the next.

On Sundays, the reminders of our past,
cause me to reflect, in bite size pieces,
but like the rain, my reflections will leave,
just as if they were never there at all.

Time

Sometimes I wish
time would stand still,
in the moments of joy,
in the laughter,
in the sharing,
in the hugs.
But it moves on,
endless, unceasing.
I try to capture
the memories,
and hold onto them
forever.

What We Found on Holiday

What we found on holiday,
was the freedom to just be,
to let go of everything,
and just be you and me.

We very soon discovered
we had a lot to say,
beyond the functionality,
that makes up every day.

We only had each other
we had no mobile phone,
we so relished the silence,
we might carry on at home.

It felt very luxurious
to have time to sit and eat.
It gave us so much freedom,
our meal times were a treat

We finally felt rested,
how much we needed sleep,
sometimes it seems the lack of it,
is what causes me to weep.

Our most important insight
was we needed time for us,
without all the distractions,
without the chaos and the fuss.

The Modern World

Stop all the texts,
remove the mobile phone,
prevent the isolation
in spending time alone,
turn off the modem,
cease the internet,
go and make some memories
you will not forget.

Let Facebook miss you,
let the tweeting stop,
go do your shopping
in an actual shop,
put down the tablet,
put the kindles back,
start living dangerously;
read a paperback!

We used to call, to just converse,
now it seems that we find nothing worse.
Talking to voicemail or to answerphone,
we have our conversations on our own.

Libraries are not wanted now,
close up every door,
dare we venture in to loiter,
or to just explore?
Losing real connection,
deprived of human touch,
face to face meetings
have become too much.

Pause

Lying still,
in the swimming pool,
going nowhere.
No one here.

Silent times,
unless I'm moving.
The water gently laps,
settling when I do.

I am at peace.
The world goes on.
Not my concern,
not right now.

Clear Ahead

Let not our yesterdays,
cloud our vision,
let our today and each tomorrow,
stand alone and count,
may we march onward,
heads held high with confidence,
knowing that everything,
passes us by.

We Cannot Live

We cannot live consumed by fear,
that is no way to live.
We hold on to ones held dear
and give what we can give.
We set about our daily lives,
though none would call us brave.
What would we do? Where would we run?
To safety or to save?

My words are easy from this place,
where I feel safe and sure.
I don't know what you've gone through,
or still have to endure.
I can turn off the radio,
or turn over my tv.
I can put the papers down,
it's just more news to me.

And yet somehow it touches us,
it's felt both far and wide,
thankful we can just carry on,
we say we're on your side.
We stand with you united,
there is no other place to be.

We are in this together,
we hope that you will see.
We're proud of you who carry on,
and do what you must do.
How would I be in your shoes?
I haven't got a clue.

Borders

They raise a wall,
we tear it down.
They start a war,
we fight for peace.
They separate,
we join together.
They teach difference,
we teach unity.

Against My Will

I came for love,
to be with the one
I couldn't live without.

Our marriage my protection,
all legal routes followed,
a citizen, a husband, a father.

Money was their God,
bosses making me complicit
in underhand dealings

The boxes left unopened,
I passed them on in silence.
I had a family to feed

I stood out, the marked man,
the recognisable face,
I was awarded the blame.

The trusted role I valued,
a mere casualty of it all,
my reputation gone.

Conviction bringing devastation,

fear, anger, remorse, and guilt
a cocktail mixed in my body.

Imprisonment for my silence,
the lesser penalty,
death, if I raised my voice.

In the alien landscape
of the empty courtroom,
our brief goodbye.

Their faces looking at me,
sad in their silence,
ingrained in my memory.

My family ripped apart.
My wife and children
living with her parents.

Yesterday I had everything,
now I have nothing,
as if it never happened.

Someone, somewhere, decided
and clanged the gate shut.
There is nothing I can do.

I am capable of love,
though it's been taken from me.

How A Scar is Made

Wounds we inflicted
lie unhealed and stinging.
Reeling from the intensity,
silence strangles my heart.

Painful examination,
the necessary evil
we must endure,
if we are to survive.

Filled with remorse,
I stand before you,
hopeful this incident
is a minor event.

Battle-Scarred

In a bed of blood
that seeped out of him,
he lay in pieces,
barely a man.

Emptiness of starvation,
unquenchable thirst,
supplies in a bag,
just out of reach.

Surrounded by the dead,
the bodies of his friends,
most no longer whole,
his fate on display,
from every angle.

His strength ebbing,
the likelihood of rescue
diminishing each minute,
he closed his eyes
and prayed.

A note with his body -
"Forgive me, I love you
always and forever."

If

If I rip my soul
into a thousand pieces,
leaving me a heap upon the ground,
then throw myself,
in wretchedness, upon your mercy
would I have your forgiveness found?

The Olive Branch

I know you think that I was wrong,
and maybe you were right,
but tell me what can be achieved
by us having a fight.

Will it alter your opinion?
Will it make me change my mind?
or is it just a situation,
that we should leave behind?

We each have said some things
that maybe we shouldn't say,
but we have got to make it up
there has to be a way.

So, I'm holding out my olive branch,
have you got yours ready yet?
I think not trying to put things right
would be cause for regret

I'm Sorry

I know we shouldn't argue,
I know we shouldn't fight,
and I know no matter what
two wrongs don't make a right.

I don't believe in violence
or hurting someone back,
I know exactly how it feels
to be under attack.

I understand the best way
of sorting problems out,
is sitting down together,
and not to scream or shout.

But sometimes our emotions
will still get in the way,
we end up saying something,
we know we shouldn't say.

It's hard to have these feelings
and keep yourself all calm.
Even though you realise
you're just doing more harm.

I wish that I could take the time
and maybe count to ten,
or go back to the beginning
and start it all again.

I don't believe in holding grudges
or harbouring regret,
so I just hope that one day
you'll manage to forget.

I hope that we are strong enough
for us to carry on,
I am sorry for everything,
am I the only one?

Sky

Sky is all we had,
just the freedom to fly,
with nothing between us,
but the ever-changing sky.

Our parachutes allowed us,
a twist on what we knew,
we saw the land before us,
from a unique point of view.

Up there we were all equal,
no one better than the rest,
all at the risk of falling,
of not being up to the test.

It was a fast descent at first,
pulling the cord, we found,
we were floating slowly,
heading gently for the ground.

Then when we safely landed,
it was so hard to believe,
the journey that we'd taken,
it was something to achieve.

As we lay there looking upward,
the plane looked so far away,
we knew whatever happened,
we would still recall this day.

The Winter Beyond My Window

Candy floss fog caressed every surface,
glistening streets, impassable in part,
the unfolding picture show mesmerising,
scenes only accessible in glimpses.

The familiar view masked an alien land,
humans had no place within,
yet here I exist,
my onlooker position offering safety,
and warmth unknown beyond these walls.

Less fortunate souls than I would navigate
this hostile, once welcoming world,
intrepid explorers in disguise,
far braver than I would ever claim to be,
would survive this place.

Dredging the details from my mind,
sadness and happiness take equal part,
I will forever cherish the day,
that winter came to me.

The Duality of The Sea

The sea is calm tonight,
I am grateful in the fading light,
that it's not using all it's might,
to worsen the ongoing fight,
to save who can be saved.

The sea is calm tonight,
at least something is going right,
after the rush and awful fright,
we must before the dark of night,
bring the survivors home.

The sea is calm tonight,
my heart is not and will not be,
until the victims are all free,
and I can very clearly see,
there's no more harm to come.

The sea is calm tonight,
there's no one left to watch but me,
to pray, to hope, to try to see,
each victim's fate or destiny,
when rescues at an end.

The sea is calm tonight,
I wish that this was all I've seen,
instead of the ongoing scene,
I wish they hadn't been so keen,
to venture out today.

The sea is calm tonight,
I see returning from the fray,
it seems the crew are all ok,
relief is mine but still I pray,
in thankfulness once more.

The sea is calm tonight.

Sometimes

Sometimes I don't know where I'm going,
sometimes I don't know where I've been.
I may not remember
the people I have seen.
Sometimes in conversation
I'll get lost along the way.
and I may not remember
the things that people say.

I try a lot of new things
I've had many times before.
I may not remember places
even when I'm through the door.
I know you, if I know you
though your name may slip my mind.
I remember if I like you,
I remember if you're kind.

If I tell you a story
I may get the facts mixed up,
but please remember in my mind
there's still a lot of stuff.
The important things stay with me
it's the little things I lose.
If you had a choice to make
now which one would you choose?

Please be patient with me
and help me if I ask.
navigating life like this
is not an easy task.
I still want to do things
and I do the best I can.
Please, don't leave me out of things,
include me in the plan.

Somewhere deep in all of this
I know that I'm still me.
Even if the things I do
make you think differently.
I may forget a lot of things
but I know this is true.
Whatever else may happen
I just want to be with you.

Keep Going

It is said we never walk alone,
I believe that this is true.
Wherever we may find ourselves,
those who love us go there too.

The road may have some twists and turns,
and we may double back,
but those who care don't leave us,
when we're under attack.

We may forget they're with us,
as they may not be in sight.
but they will always be there,
when we really need to fight.

So, if at times the tides are rough,
when they come rolling in,
remember you are not alone,
you don't have to give in.

Navigation

Human relationships are complicated.
We navigate them through choppy waters
and across the sea of calm.

We feel abandoned, alone, isolated,
loved, cosseted, wanted,
fragile, strong, unsure.

We choose our words,
or they come without thinking,
our actions too at times.

We let others dictate,
or we stand independent,
come what may.

We sometimes debate the value,
against the risk of letting go.
We need, we want, we love

That Precious Moment

That precious moment
when first I held you,
and the lightness of your being
fused with the heaviness of mine,
it was as if, from that moment,
sense and responsibility
and all that entails,
was thrust into my world,
to change it forever.

With each and every detail
of my life altered by
this one addition,
this person's entrance,
into an otherwise peaceful life,
I closed my eyes,
and although paralysed
with your very weight,
I understood.

This was a sign,
a message was being sent,
that this was a new beginning,
that this was the end of
what might have been.

Here and now
was who I hoped I would become.
Somewhere in my heart of hearts
I had longed for this moment,
this progression into the adult world.

You Know Who You Are

I never thought it would happen,
that someone I had never met
would become so important to me,
would really be my friend,
yet here we are.

I have shared my stories with you
my hopes, my fears,
and you have respected my trust.
When I get scared, wanting to run,
you reassure me that I am safe.

I feel l have known you forever,
this connection we share
seems beyond explanation.
To have this multiple times over,
the odds astound me.

I am braver because of you.
I am stronger because of you.
I am more me than I ever was
because of you, all of you.
I salute you in your royalty.

Oh You

In the beginning
I didn't expect anything.
This was another course,
another qualification,
just online.
I was so wrong.
I cannot express
my gratitude enough.

People I may never meet
have had my back.
They have taught me, showed me,
helped me, supported me,
been there for me
when times were difficult
and when I was too.

I have learnt so much
beyond the modules,
the coursework, and tutorials
because of their patience,
their understanding,
their willingness to accept me
for who I am.
This group of people

have collectively and individually
become so important to me,
that I am forever grateful
I took the chance
to get to know them.

I am so lucky and grateful
that they took a chance on me,
and let me be their friend.

Forever

If time shall come,
when my presence
becomes unwanted,
I will remove myself
at your request.

But still there is
a corner of my heart,
that shall forever
belong to you,
whatever may befall.

For love is always love
if it is true.
Your absence
would cause me sorrow,
but never shall I mourn.

You will to me
forever live.
So, you shall never die
as long as breath
remains in me.

No Tears

No tears, no confetti,
no sparkling champagne,
it's just you and me,
together again.

No limo, no flowers,
nothing to explain,
just us together,
and starting again.

No wedding day jitters,
no rings to exchange,
no music to dance to,
nothing to arrange.

Why can't people get it?
I love you that's all,
I don't want to change it,
we're having a ball.

There's A Very Pleasant Feeling

There's a very pleasant feeling
watching water rushing by,
in quiet observation,
as the sun ascends the sky.

There's something about the way
it carries life within its flow,
that brings thoughts of you closer
I can't bear to let them go.

I think of times we spent together
and it breaks my heart in two,
that the turning of the tide
has taken me away from you.

Just a stream of flowing water
as it makes its way alone,
if the strength within that river
had only been my own.

In quiet observation,
as the sun ascends the sky,
there's a very pleasant feeling
watching water rushing by.

Fragility

Your love for me and your expression of it,
reaches into the depths of my soul.
I feel encapsulated by its existence,
I am helpless to resist its power.
I desire you and hunger for you
more than any food or drink,
and it sustains me night and day.
I am astounded by its plentiful supply
despite my unceasing consumption.
I cannot return such love,
I have not the resources
to meet like with like.
It seems inevitable that it will end,
as love like yours deserves much more,
than a broken person such as me can offer.

A Memory?

She closed her eyes and dreamed a while
her face took on a grin.
She watched the moving images
and they were all of him.

No voices heard, she felt no touch,
yet she could sense him near.
Was this the thing called love?
that many paid the price of dear.

The darkness never ending,
her solitude magnified.
How many nights had she lain sleeping?
How many tears had she cried?

Her heart it lay in pieces,
scattered all upon the floor.
As it had been on that night
when he had walked out the door.

Would she ever, could she ever
feel once more whole again?
Would this go on forever?
Would things always be the same?

Then as daylight broke, she saw him,
looking real as he could be.
Was it a dim and distant picture
of a fading memory?

The Love of My Life

They say the first year is the hardest,
It's a little early for me to say,
I won't pretend it's been easy,
but I wouldn't have it any other way.

If it didn't hurt sometimes,
then it wouldn't be so real,
but losing you the way I did,
well I can't say how I feel.

There have been times,
when I longed to fall into your arms,
not the arms of another.

When your voice could have soothed
and I searched for your words.

When you would have made me laugh,
yet crying was all I could do.

When I needed to see you
and all I had was a photograph.

Make no mistake
this is not goodbye,
that could never be.
As long as I live in this world
you will be with me.

The Spaces In-Between

We have our moments good and bad,
the things that really make us sad,
the happy times that we can share,
can make us somehow more aware,
we love each other
in the spaces in-between.

The testing times that we've been through,
through everything I still had you.
Sometimes it's mundane that is true,
I would be nothing without you,
we love each other
in the spaces in-between.

I feel your sorrow and your pain,
you sometimes don't have to explain,
it's the difference that you make,
without you I think I would break,
we love each other
in the spaces in-between.

My happiness it comes from you,
the little things you say and do,
I thank my stars most every night,
that I have you to hold me tight,
we love each other
in the spaces in-between.

You

You're the sun in the morning,
you're the stars in the sky,
you're raindrops on my window,
you're the wind rushing by.

You're the moon as it's rising,
you're the first fall of snow,
you will always be with me,
every place that I go.

Vegas

By the time I get to Vegas I'll be 60,
been standing in the airport line so long.
By the time I get to Vegas I'll be 60,
I'm thinking it might be where I belong.

By the time I get to Vegas I'll be 70,
at least I'll have my pension pot to spend.
By the time I get to Vegas I'll be 70,
Wondering if my clothes will be on trend.

By the time I get to Vegas I'll be 80,
I reckon that I'll still walk the walk
By the time I get to Vegas I'll be 80,
mind, saying that, I could be all talk.

By the time I get to Vegas I'll be 90,
the bright lights might be too much for me.
By the time I get to Vegas I'll be 90,
the chances are that I'll need company.

By the time I get to Vegas I'll be 100,
either that or I might be dead.
By the time I get to Vegas I'll be 100,
I will probably have forgotten what I said.

What Happened?

It's a miserable Monday
in yesterday's clothes,
I'm telling you now,
I don't smell like a rose,
I'm aching all over,
did I get in a fight?
Something tells me
this isn't quite right.

My eyes are hurting,
why is it so bright?
When there's only me here
to turn on the light
The room is spinning,
who is doing that?
I know it's not me,
so it must be the cat.

There's a takeaway carton
right there by my feet,
so at least now I know
I had something to eat.
I reach for a tab
but the packet is empty,
it was full last night
so, I must have smoked twenty.

I can see my jacket
and also my shoes.
What happened last night?
I am searching for clues.
Guinness and whisky
that's quite a mix,
it seems like last night
I was up to old tricks.

I know it's important
that I take a shower,
but I just need to lie here,
still, for an hour.
I need the bathroom
and I need it quick,
the rise in my throat says
I'm going to be sick.

My phone won't stop buzzing,
the rumours are rife
Oh, why won't some people
get out of my life?
When I recover
I will sort through it all,
exactly what happened,
I cannot recall.

Words, Words, Words

Was it to be or not to be?
Were the ides of March a fantasy?
Was it on Twelfth Night it came to be?
Did Macbeth a dagger see?
When Juliet found her Romeo
why did they not take heed and go?
The Tempest raged, brought the terrors,
it was just a Comedy of Errors.
If time means that Love's Labour's Lost
take a Midsummer Dream, hang the cost
Was it King John or was it King Lear?
The one that made the people cheer
Not Desdemona with Othello.
Was she ever with this fellow?
I feel the force of a Winter's Tale,
looking like my time to bail.

A Poet's "Thank You"

I am proud to be a Poet,
it's part of my identity,
my writing default position,
and medium of expression,
it's my form of communication.

It is raw, it is vulnerable,
it is putting me on the page.
My words put up for scrutiny,
a glimpse into my soul,
by people known and unknown.

It has been met with disregard,
silenced, forgotten, abandoned.
It bears no grudge, sits patiently,
waiting on my invitation,
for that, I am truly grateful.

Now you've read my book
don't forget to review
Amazon, Goodreads,
Bookbub too!
Thank you very much
I'm counting on you!

Lily x

Acknowledgements

I am incredibly lucky in my life to have people who inspire me and support me. I have met lots of people who have read poems, offered advice, and encouraged me. I would love to say thank you individually to all of them and to everyone who follows me on Twitter, Facebook, Instagram lilyswritinglife.com or lilylawson.com but that would be a book itself. If you are reading this and you are one of those people, I thank you.

I will single out some of them.

Keith Roper for providing the photograph for the cover of this book.

Christine Hutchinson for her infinite patience, her unwavering support, her wisdom and for the mantra "no wasted words" which I hope has been applied within this book. I am honoured to be her friend.

Anita Ralhan, gorgeous human, for her endless support and friendship. She lifts my spirits with her care and her cheerleading. The strength of her belief makes me want to keep reaching and challenging myself.

Ann Garcia for her generosity of spirit and her honesty. She inspires me with her poetry and her writing to reach into myself and push my boundaries as a poet and a writer. I value all she has taught me. This is a better book because of her and her feedback. I am braver and stronger because of her.

Cairistìona Màiri MacEòin, the title Queen, for giving some of these poems' titles. I appreciate her teaching about poetic form, her patience in choosing fonts and her ever-welcome artistic, critical eye. But most of all for her compassion, understanding and advice.

Cin McGuigan for being supportive of my poetry and supplying the prompts which led to some of the poems in this book. I greatly appreciate her unlimited virtual hugs, her wise counsel, and her belief in me. I am grateful for her friendship and her encouragement.

Adele Sullivan for critiquing this book, for her encouragement, advice, support, care, and compassion. She has taught me so much and I am thankful to have her in my life.

Tracy Hutchinson, my first writer friend and my first friend on Twitter. Her friendship, compassion and understanding is very special to me.

Kate Brazier for critiquing this book, for pushing me to do better, and believing that I could. I am grateful for all the "nit picking" that helped make this book what it is. I cherish her compassion, understanding and friendship.

Louise Wilford for the prompts that led to some of the poems in this book, and for her tolerance of my many drafts of those poems. She inspires me to share my poetry.

Suzanne Burn for expanding my knowledge of poetic form, for critiquing individual poems and the versions of this book with patience and generosity. I cherish her friendship and her understanding.

And finally, my parents for everything they have done for me and given me. Their belief in my poetry means so much.

By The Author

My Father's Daughter

'My Father's Daughter, a collection of poems ranging from light-hearted to heart-rending captures Lily Lawson's thoughtful observations about life and love.'

A Taste of What's to Come

A selection of accessible, relatable, eclectic poetry. Each piece tells its story in only the way Lily can.'

Rainbow's Red Book of Poetry

Weaving through love and hate,
I rise from the ashes, my words you own –
I am red.

**Something different,
an illustrated children's book.**

Santa's Early Christmas

Last year Santa was hungry and thirsty by the time he delivered all the presents. But when he came home there was no food and drink left! This year Santa decides things are going to be different.

A poem from
Rainbow's Red Book of Poetry

Hate vs Love

Hate leaks from lips,
its powerful punch poisoning all within its wake,
wasting weighty words on trivial pursuits.

Love flows from the heart,
its calming lotion pouring in caressing streams,
healing wounds, seeping into souls.

Hate's afflicted admirers
keen to ingratiate themselves
bow and scrape at its feet.
When they hear the battle cry, they charge.

Love listens long.
Its gentle voice persuading, reaching out,
accepting all in its embrace.

About The Author

Lily Lawson is a poet and fiction writer living in the UK. She has poetry, short stories and creative non-fiction published in anthologies and online in addition to her books.

You can find out more about Lily and read more of her work on her blog. Subscribers to Life with Lily are the first to hear all her writing news. You can sign up here.

Printed in Great Britain
by Amazon

16798517R00066